BOOKSHOP
Phonics
Intervention
Partner Practice Book

MONDO
PUBLISHING

For information contact:

MONDO Publishing
980 Avenue of the Americas
New York NY 10018

Visit our website at www.mondopub.com

Printed in China

09 10 11 12 13   9 8 7 6 5 4 3 2 1

ISBN 978-1-60175-426-4

Design by Witz End Design

Write, Sound, and Say Words

1. *fast* 2. *fat* 3. *pat*

4. *am* 5. _____ 6. _____

_____ _____ _____

Read Carefully

happy	at	little	fat
pat	the	Sam	am
at	fast	happy	is
see	I	am	fast

Write, Sound, and Say Words

1. here   2. map   3. are

4. _____   5. _____   6. _____

_____   _____   _____

Read Carefully

☑

my	map	little	sat
pass	the	pat	is
here	look	Sam	fast
tap	mat	happy	are
see	am	at	to

☑

Write, Sound, and Say Words

1. pan   2. are   3. if

4. happy   5. happy   6.

Read Carefully

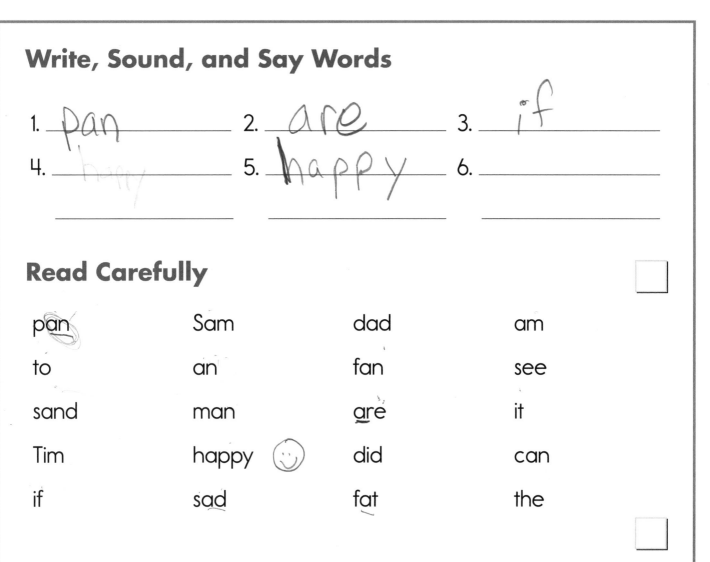

pan	Sam	dad	am
to	an	fan	see
sand	man	are	it
Tim	happy	did	can
if	sad	fat	the

Write, Sound, and Say Words

1. _____ 2. _____ 3. _____

4. _____ 5. _____ 6. _____

_____ _____ _____

Read Carefully

fit	miss	past	little
here	pat	my	nap
tip	sad	in	and
cap	is	ant	sit
sand	pin	Tim	look
sat	tap	did	pan

Write, Sound, and Say Words

1. _____ 2. _____ 3. _____

4. _____ 5. _____ 6. _____

_____ _____ _____

Read Carefully

did	if	fast	and
man	happy	am	here
miss	Dan	cat	dad
at	sand	pan	it
past	are	see	sat
little	can	in	Pam

Write, Sound, and Say Words

1. _____   2. _____   3. _____

4. _____   5. _____   6. _____

_____   _____   _____

Read Carefully

sand	sat	Tim	been
have	lift	had	miss
man	said	fast	soft
sit	past	of	fan
from	Dan	sad	mom
hill	hand	fin	Don

Write, Sound, and Say Words

1. _____ 2. _____ 3. _____

4. _____ 5. _____ 6. _____

_____ _____ _____

Read Carefully

from	you	doll	of
last	pass	hand	list
Tim	have	gift	they
come	lost	Tom	land
lift	pot	been	had
said	has	past	were

Write, Sound, and Say Words

1. _____   2. _____   3. _____

4. _____   5. _____   6. _____

_____   _____   _____

Read Carefully

come	ask	did	you
lamp	they	hot	bag
ship	kick	dip	were
dot	has	fish	dad
hat	big	lap	hop
back	shop	from	mask

Write, Sound, and Say Words

1. _____   2. _____   3. _____

4. _____   5. _____   6. _____

_____   _____   _____

Read Carefully

soft	sick	had	pot
they	kid	lot	said
got	been	kit	pick
hand	off	from	log
has	lost	sock	have
pack	dog	of	and

Write, Sound, and Say Words

1. _____ 2. _____ 3. _____

4. _____ 5. _____ 6. _____

_____ _____ _____

Read Carefully

on	pick	band	hill
come	bad	ask	have
dish	rock	were	lick
back	of	ship	him
lock	tag	shall	you
been	fish	said	shop

Write, Sound, and Say Words

1. _____ 2. _____ 3. _____ 4. _____

5. _____ 6. _____ 7. _____ 8. _____

_____ _____ _____ _____

Read Carefully

been	land	back	any
put	have	bed	dig
bet	does	lift	sick
lad	him	bag	best
like	lost	of	there
big	list	sack	last

Read the Story

Bob and Jill went to shop for socks.

"I like soft socks," said Bob. "Look. Here is a big bag of soft socks."

"I like red socks," said Jill. "Here is a little bag of red socks."

Bob and Jill put the bags of socks in a big sack. They left the shop. Bob's dog, Tag, grabbed the sack and ran.

"Come back here!" yelled Bob. Tag ran back. He dropped the sack. Bob petted Tag.

Write, Sound, and Say Words

1. _____ 2. _____ 3. _____ 4. _____

5. _____ 6. _____ 7. _____ 8. _____

_____ _____ _____ _____

Read Carefully

pick	good	there	want
any	ask	gift	shop
back	from	on	like
of	do	was	pack
does	off	lamp	let
pet	put	left	who

Read the Story

Jim and Tom are on a ship. The ship is rocking.

"I am sick," said Jim. "I want the ship to quit rocking!"

"Sit on the deck and rest," said Tom. "That will help."

The ship stopped. Jim and Tom stepped on the ramp and then on sand.

"It is good to be on land!" said Jim.

Write, Sound, and Say Words

1. _____ 2. _____ 3. _____ 4. _____

5. _____ 6. _____ 7. _____ 8. _____

_____ _____ _____ _____

Read Carefully

quack	hot	want	they
does	wet	net	with
said	any	this	was
were	has	and	hit
west	quick	you	there
hand	hat	who	job

Read the Story

"Can you help my pets?" Kim asked the vet. "My dog is sick. My cat has a cut on its leg, and my duck will not quack."

"Yes. I can help your pets," said the vet.

The vet fixed the cut on the cat. Then the vet said, "This shot will help your dog." The vet put the duck in a pen with six ducks. They quacked and quacked.

"You are the best vet!" said Kim.

Write, Sound, and Say Words

1. _____ 2. _____ 3. _____ 4. _____

5. _____ 6. _____ 7. _____ 8. _____

_____ _____ _____ _____

Read Carefully

good	red	big	box
help	sock	does	do
dig	put	that	sand
hill	wig	like	bag
rock	sack	dog	does
any	come	quit	want

Read the Story

I was napping in my tent when a big wind grabbed it. I ran to get it and slipped on the wet rocks. I fell on a rock. I got a gash on my leg. The tent landed in the sand. I yelled for Mom and Dad. They came quick! Mom fixed my leg. Dad got my tent.

"That does it!" I said. "My next nap is in my bed!"

Write, Sound, and Say Words

1. _____ 2. _____ 3. _____ 4. _____

5. _____ 6. _____ 7. _____ 8. _____

_____   _____   _____   _____

Read Carefully

who	soft	list	let
yet	like	wish	lift
mom	last	there	hand
good	leg	hop	cost
fox	pet	next	left
do	want	were	put

Read the Story

A little red hen was in a box. There was a net on the top of the box.

"I wish the net was not on this box," said the little red hen. "I want to run and hop."

The little red hen pecked at the net. Then the net fell off the box. The little red hen ran and hopped.

"Well," said the little red hen, "I am a happy little hen. I like to run and hop."

Write, Sound, and Say Words

1. _____ 2. _____ 3. _____ 4. _____

5. _____ 6. _____ 7. _____ 8. _____

_____ _____ _____ _____

Read Carefully

hand	no	your	slip
me	just	tagged	very
find	had	run	ripping
want	rested	spill	be
when	door	go	ran
step	spell	fish	as
picks	does	bed	my

Read the Story

Ken and Dan want to go to the top of the big hill. Ken packs a map. Dan packs a big snack. Ken and Dan go up the hill.

"I want to stop and look at my map," said Ken.

"I want my snack," said Dan.

"No, Dan, we can have a snack when we get to the top of the hill," said Ken.

Ken and Dan got to the top and then had a snack. It was good.

Write, Sound, and Say Words

1. _____   2. _____   3. _____   4. _____

5. _____   6. _____   7. _____   8. _____

_____   _____   _____   _____

Read Carefully

many	sand	into	men
want	one	them	lifted
as	end	naps	this
then	mud	very	went
spell	napping	where	go
his	he	sun	door
resting	your	find	jump

Read the Story

I cannot find my mittens. I looked in the basket next to the door. No mittens. I asked Gus if he had my mittens.

Gus said, "No, I do not have your mittens."

I was getting very upset! Where are my mittens?

"Did you look in your jacket pocket?" asked Gus.

I looked in my pocket. There were my mittens!

Write, Sound, and Say Words

1. _____ 2. _____ 3. _____ 4. _____

5. _____ 6. _____ 7. _____ 8. _____

_____ _____ _____ _____

Read Carefully

chop	your	fills	camp
very	landed	find	begging
hopped	spun	any	put
many	one	van	his
lick	we	that	then
went	as	ten	much
pet	than	when	want

Read the Story

Jack is my little kitten. Jack was napping on my bed.

"Get off that bed!" yelled my Mom.

Jack ran and hid.

"Come back, Jack," I said.

Then Jack ran in. He did a big jump. He landed in my lap and licked my chin. "Jack, you are the best cat! But stop jumping on my bed."

Write, Sound, and Say Words

1. _____ 2. _____ 3. _____ 4. _____

5. _____ 6. _____ 7. _____ 8. _____

_____ _____ _____ _____

Read Carefully

than	into	who	spot
not	went	door	rested
your	lift	then	no
ripping	picked	where	many
find	mops	want	when
shut	there	past	filled
smell	his	lump	stack

Read the Story

There are six mugs in the box. Stan has a red mug. Pam has a little mug with a duck on it. Don has a big mug that looks like a pumpkin. Ben has a mug with a fish. Dot and Dan have mugs with dogs.

"I have the best mug," said Chad. "My mug has CHAD on it!"

Write, Sound, and Say Words

1. _____ 2. _____ 3. _____ 4. _____

5. _____ 6. _____ 7. _____ 8. _____

_____ _____ _____ _____

Read Carefully

hummed	as	red	door
stuck	dusted	went	sitting
mask	gum	jumped	stopping
one	slip	with	when
was	then	step	where
hugged	very	dust	want
them	tell	into	stick

Read the Story

Bob had cash to spend. He wanted to spend it on gifts. He went to the gift shop. He got Kim a doll, and he got Jeff a cup. He got Dad a clock and Mom a dish of mints. He put the gifts in red bags. He handed the bags to Kim, Jeff, Dad, and Mom.

Mom handed Bob a red bag. "This gift is for you!" said Mom.

Bob was happy.

Read Carefully

game	went	about	stacks
spot	stopped	path	but
away	cake	run	dusted
rocket	two	upon	just
log	name	running	when
bus	spotted	some	pins
spelled	which	leg	cut
spin	fun	napkin	want

Read the Story

Jake was at camp. His dog Rex was missing! It was a puzzle.

"I spotted your dog running away," said Ben. "Did you look at the lake?"

Jake ran up the path. Rex was not on the path. He ran to the lake, but Rex was not at the lake. Just when Jake was about to run back to the camp, he came to a cave. He went in the cave. There was Rex, taking a nap!

"Rex!" yelled Jake. Rex jumped up and ran to Jake.

"I am so glad to see you!" said Jake.

Read Carefully

rabbit	away	until	four
chop	rack	your	stopped
hands	jump	about	made
rake	them	came	some
pretty	spell	other	handed
just	still	late	stem
make	jumping	duck	two
carry	then	find	same

Read the Story

"Oh, look at these dolls," said Ann. "Can I have one, Mom?"

"I think you can have one on your next *birthday*. Which one do you want?" asked Mom.

"I like the one in the pretty pink dress. It is the best one," said Ann.

At last it was Ann's birthday. Ann still wanted the doll with the pretty pink dress.

Mom and Dad came in with a big box. "Happy Birthday, Ann!" they said.

Ann looked in the box. It was the doll with the pink dress. Ann was very happy!

Read Carefully

we	skin	way	stopping
stay	jumped	pretty	than
about	ate	such	other
Stan	some	very	picnic
rested	ran	stain	pail
must	play	two	lifted
spell	that	wagging	take
pocket	much	jumps	four

Read the Story

I am planning a trip. I will go to the *airport*. A plane will take me away. There will be a train waiting for me. The train will take me to a big ship. I will sit on the ship and nap. The ship will sail away to a place with sun and sand. There will be lots of *water*.

I can play in the sand and swim in the water. I cannot wait to go on my big trip.

Read Carefully

wait	do	frogs	us
away	up	pretty	wind
jumping	yes	went	picked
wish	swim	nail	two
running	about	go	kitten
happen	lake	who	sun
carry	be	this	swam
taps	want	paint	with

Read the Story

We are helping Dad paint the *fence*. We have buckets of paint, brushes, and rags.

We paint the fence. Dad paints the gate. It looks fine, but the paint is still wet.

Muffin, Miss White's cat, runs to the wet fence. He gets paint on him! Miss White will be mad. I will get the paint off with a rag. There are still spots. I will rub them off and carry Muffin back to Miss White.

Read Carefully

where	shipping	test	away
shopping	day	he	skill
other	Jake	well	pain
landed	where	frame	carry
Jack	four	paint	door
bell	his	slammed	no
gave	mopped	into	were
one	me	bath	hopped

Read the Story

It is raining. Max and Jane have to stay in. What can they do?

"Let's bake a cake!" said Jane. I will get the box of cake mix and a can of frosting."

Max and Jane mixed the cake. They baked it in a pan.

"The cake is hot," said Max. "We do not want the frosting to melt. Let's play a game while we wait."

They played a game and then went to check on the cake.

"It is not hot," said Jane.

Max and Jane frosted the cake and ate it.

"Yum!" they said.

Read Carefully

find	plain	bike	plans
give	bottle	because	dripped
sudden	cake	door	apple
bundle	blessing	blade	flash
planned	very	what	gave
life	battle	bring	middle
sail	spotless	ride	your
again	game	jacket	traffic

Read the Story

We are *having* a picnic today. I have a big picnic basket. We will put a blanket on the grass here in the shade. Then we will take a hike and have our lunch. We have *sandwiches* and cake. We have apples. We have drinks in bottles. Yum! This will be a fun picnic.

Wait! Look at the ants on the blanket. They will go into the basket. Stop! We will put our basket in this spot. A spot with no ants!

Read Carefully

drive	think	give	dimple
carry	their	light	shifted
again	cry	puzzle	came
cattle	please	four	side
winning	planning	him	what
why	ate	rain	thing
prize	your	drink	into
many	because	candle	say

Read the Story

"Mom," called Liz.

"What is it?" asked Mom.

"I cannot nap," said Liz.

"You must rest," said Mom. "Is the light too bright?"

"No, the light is just right," said Liz.

"Are you sick?" asked Mom.

"No, I am fine," said Liz.

"We will look at a book," said Mom.

Mom and Liz looked at a book. When she finished, Mom asked Liz if she liked the book. Liz was very still. She was napping!

Read Carefully

unlock	one	give	other
fumble	please	picked	pile
fine	want	simple	into
again	takes	may	fiddle
wrap	stay	pretty	make
jumped	their	were	what
cuddle	jumps	running	class
where	train	pumpkin	resting

Read the Story

We had a play. *Parents* came to see the play. The lights came up. They were bright!

Pam had a pretty white dress. She sang a song. I juggled plates. I tossed them up high and did not drop one!

Bill played the fiddle. He was very good. Five children tapped. They tapped fast and did not stumble.

At the end of the play, we made a line. We all sang while Bill played a song. The parents clapped. They liked our play!

Read Carefully

paint	ripping	their	away
because	until	white	tray
claim	high	kettle	give
grumble	what	try	hopped
pocket	flight	why	write
into	way	name	tagged
landed	some	hopping	juggle
take	blushing	day	tested

Read the Story

Fire! Fire! A fire was coming across the grass. It was getting very hot! The men and *women* rushed to stop the fire.

Crack! A big branch fell. Run to a safe spot! The fire was strong! The men and women had buckets.

They made a chain and passed the buckets in the line. They battled the blaze, but in the end, they stopped the fire. The men and women were very brave!

Name _____

Read Carefully

brag	clapping	flash	because
tickle	two	stumble	while
again	nine	night	upon
clay	give	way	struggle
hair	right	please	tested
their	tackle	about	fire
white	insect	bragged	tablet
crushed	pair	rabbit	why

Read the Story

The *baseball* game was in the last inning. The score was 2 to 2. The Big Cats were at bat. The bases were full.

Dan hit a high one, but Mike stopped the play. Next came Bill. He did not get a hit.

Then came Jim. Jim swung the bat and hit the ball with a big crack! It was a home run! The fans yelled as Jim crossed home plate.

What a game!

Read Carefully

close	blank	stone	while
trumpet	give	has	long
would	stepped	home	thank
shone	bike	happen	should
have	skip	time	stumble
cry	stand	hope	were
think	white	before	by
black	swim	could	sang

Read the Story

Bubbles the *hamster* had a happy life. He had a big home with a gate. There was lots of stuff to nibble.

One day, the door on his home was left *open*. "What would it be like to run in the grass?" said Bubbles. He hopped and ran to the door.

"Not so fast," said Kim the cat. "I think a hamster would make a good snack."

Bubbles ran back to his home. He jumped in and slammed the door. "I think grass is not very safe!" he said.

Read Carefully

rabbit	plain	buy	would
there	what	pickle	fly
should	boat	were	some
traffic	planned	away	grow
dress	could	hike	drop
fight	kept	coat	hers
both	pocket	where	jumble
stepping	broke	plane	cold

Read the Story

It was very hot.

"Let's give the dog a bath," Rose said to Joan. "It will take both of us to do the job." They pulled the dog to the tub.

"Hold him!" said Joan. "I will get the soap."

Joan went inside, but she did not see the soap in the box. "There is no soap," said Joan.

"The dog did not want a bath," said Rose. "He ran away, so I'm soaking in the tub. It is very cold."

Joan and Rose were happy. They were no *longer* hot!

Read Carefully

drumming	other	basket	both
song	puzzle	five	blend
would	grinned	again	fine
hold	grass	high	picnic
hers	fire	west	should
want	old	buy	riddle
rabbit	could	spray	light
twist	own	went	float

Read the Story

Dad slipped on the path. He could not get up. "Help, help!" he called. Old Man Jones came up the path.

"Please get my wife!" said Dad.

"No," said Old Man Jones. "I do not have a knife."

"I want my wife!" said Dad.

"Yes, I do have a good life," said Old Man Jones.

"I slipped," said Dad, "and my back is not right."

"Well, have a good trip," said Old Man Jones. "See you *tomorrow* night!"

Just then Mom came up the path. "Thank you for helping," Mom said to Old Man Jones. Dad just sighed.

Read Carefully

hers	road	thank	knot
rabbit	could	drink	like
running	pocket	buy	sang
pretty	think	because	both
packed	please	show	brushed
would	life	popped	might
blink	pebble	told	thing
myself	sing	should	drummed

Read the Story

Brad had a pet rabbit named Hops. Hops was a pretty black and white rabbit. He could jump very high and run very fast. Hops liked to nibble apples.

One day, Hops was hopping very fast. He did not look where he was hopping. He hopped right in a bucket of paint. What a mess!

Brad picked Hops up. He rubbed him with soap. He sprayed him with *water*. It was not long until Hops's coat shined.

Hops still likes to hop very fast, but he *watches* for paint buckets!

Read Carefully

could	into	right	both
shine	bring	buy	line
prize	why	know	upset
crushed	shone	side	should
blow	about	swimming	night
hers	simple	their	brushing
children	glow	spring	ride
sudden	would	try	slammed

Read the Story

Pickles was a puppet. He had a big red smile. He put on a show for children. Pickles told jokes and sang songs with a little help from the man holding his strings.

One day, Pickles fell. He broke his *head*. There was a crack on his face. "Do not be sad. I know just what to do," said the man who pulled the strings. He fixed the crack. He painted a big red smile.

Pickles went back to making the children happy. The show was a lot of fun!

Read Carefully

goal	cases	live	beep
feet	would	driving	brushed
pebble	glasses	coast	know
most	tree	white	clean
hidden	drove	could	grape
flipping	brushes	running	kind
should	Steve	soak	paddle
while	making	both	knight

Read the Story

"I wish I had a whole *barrel* of peanuts," said Pete. "I would mash them up to make peanut butter."

"I wish I had a bunch of grapes," said Tad, "I would put grapes in a pan to make grape jam."

"We are set," said Pete.

"Not quite," said Tad. "What will we put it on?"

Just then Mom came home. "I have a treat," said Mom. "A bag of bagels."

"Just what we need!" said Pete and Tad.

They put peanut butter and jam on the bagels. Yum!

Read Carefully

plain	nice	kind	baking
glow	glasses	place	buzzes
ropes	live	friend	show
pray	dropping	ice	prizes
goes	green	named	brushes
clock	frosting	hear	told
gnome	gray	poked	know
handed	o'clock	planted	most

Read the Story

Dave liked to *dance*. When the band played, Dave would start tapping his feet. "This band has a good beat," said Dave. "I like that song a lot."

Dave asked Joan to dance. They danced all the fast ones. They danced until nine o'clock.

"I have to go home, Dave," said Joan.

"Thanks for the dances, Joan," said Dave. "I would like to dance with you again. Could you meet me here next week?"

"I will be here next week," said Joan. "We will just keep on dancing!"

Read Carefully

riding	hold	race	goes
kind	sharp	striped	stink
hopped	riddle	buy	prizes
please	live	start	hoping
share	hers	fire	friend
what	raking	again	bark
o'clock	old	places	own
drink	stare	most	piled

Read the Story

Ted's class went on a trip to a farm to pick apples. Farmer Jones met the class at the gate.

"Here are baskets," said Farmer Jones. "You may each have one basket, and you can each pick six apples."

Ted looked for six red apples. He saw six good apples in the green leaves. "I wish I could reach them," said Ted.

"Here you go, Ted," said Farmer Jones. "I will reach them and hand them to you."

"Thanks! I will give them to my mom," said Ted. "She will make a *great* apple pie!"

Read Carefully

live	sheep	grumble	before
think	brushes	sweet	griping
framed	busted	timing	goes
part	kind	coat	taping
stumble	winning	because	hard
o'clock	please	friend	lifted
street	grow	hiding	crashes
thank	tapping	park	most

Read the Story

Robin and Bob were skating on the ice. It was cold, but skating helped to warm them up.

"Wait," called Robin. "I lost a mitten in the snow."

Bob stopped to help Robin.

"It is a *special* mitten," said Robin. "My mom knitted it for me."

They looked for the mitten until it started to get dark.

"We should go home, Robin," said Bob.

Robin felt like she would cry. Just then she saw a flash of red. She skated to the snow bank. There was the lost mitten.

"Okay, let's go home!" said Robin.

Read Carefully

shark	leave	car	picking
goes	liked	kind	home
care	their	graded	year
sleep	hope	start	most
live	thank	why	stand
joking	friend	scream	think
stare	frame	o'clock	tickle
farm	glasses	each	closes

Read the Story

I know a tale of two knights of old.

One knight was shy, and the other was bold.

White knight told tall tales of his battles and fights.

Black knight did not brag and kept out of sight—

Until the day came when a *dragon* came near.

Black knight was brave, and white knight quaked in fear.

Being brave isn't just what you want others to hear.

Being brave also means facing your fears.

Read Carefully

bee	taping	head	faces
pickle	bright	bark	hops
know	what	white	almost
while	brake	here	fact
keep	eyes	tapping	peanut
picnic	show	want	dark
why	barn	brushes	because
hopes	clean	bank	blue

Read the Story

"What are you reading?" asked Pete.

"I'm reading a *mystery*," said Steve.

"What's it about?" asked Pete.

"The queen's gold coins are missing," said Steve. "I don't mean to be rude, but I'm on the last page of the book. I have the clues. I almost know who did it."

"I read that book last week," said Pete.

"Please don't tell me the end!" screamed Steve.

"Got it," said Pete. "I should not tell you that the maid stole the coins and hid them in the tree."

"Thanks, Pete," sighed Steve.

Read Carefully

tunnel	dear	shark	farm
most	head	use	races
street	leave	hers	grow
prizes	joked	share	eyes
would	almost	knot	live
goat	each	ice	boat
spray	tune	stumble	place
sharp	told	far	share

Read the Story

"Get up, Jill," called Mom. "It's eight o'clock."

"My bed is all nice and soft," said Jill.

Dad was tapping on the door. "Come on, Jill," called Dad. "We'll be late."

"My eyes are shut tight," said Jill.

"Get your clothes on," called Mom.

"I'll get the car," said Dad.

"I want to stay home from school," said Jill.

"There is no school today," called Mom. "We're taking a trip to the beach."

Jill hopped right out of bed. "Let's go!" she said.

Read Carefully

riddle	ear	buy	coat
school	ride	cold	eyes
drank	or	black	knight
licked	eight	eat	blast
trade	liked	head	hard
almost	fruit	road	most
blank	three	dark	for
coast	track	tree	clothes

Read the Story

It was a pretty day in June.

"This is a good day for a picnic," said Jean.

"Let's pack a basket," said Sue.

"I'll get the fruit, drinks, and corn chips," said Jean.

"I'll get the hot dogs and pickles," said Sue.

When they left the house, the sky was getting dark.
Then it started raining.

"Oh, no," said Jean. "What can we do?"

"I know," said Sue. "We could have our picnic on the porch!"

Jean and Sue had a fun picnic on the porch.

Read Carefully

please	start	hopped	head
bubble	same	could	suit
feet	almost	star	need
clue	trumpet	kind	hoped
eyes	park	year	short
sport	live	candle	clothes
hear	own	stare	rule
spotted	green	their	crashes

Read the Story

James is in the school band. He plays the trumpet. The band concert is next week.

"I need a suit to *wear* to the concert," said James. "My old suit doesn't fit. The pants and sleeves are too short."

"I'll buy you a suit," said Dad.

Dad and James went to the store. They got a blue suit for James to wear at the concert.

James looked quite sharp wearing his blue suit and playing the trumpet.

Read Carefully

read	tray	almost	tickle
thank	between	flat	sang
try	friend	hear	eight
school	old	north	storm
float	song	hopping	seen
should	clothes	tackle	goes
sing	think	see	classes
seem	hoping	into	hold

Read the Story

Liz likes to sing all day long. She likes to sing happy songs, sad songs, and just about any song you can think of.

"When I'm bigger," said Liz, "I want to be a singing star. All my fans will clap and cheer when I sing. I'll have on *sparkly* clothes. I'll stand on *stage* in the bright lights. It'll be so much fun!"

Mom came into Liz's room. "It's time to pick up your clothes and clean off your desk."

"Oh, well," said Liz. "I can dream while I clean!"

Read Carefully

train	lakes	blue	bang
should	bird	can't	hers
stain	buy	licked	subject
bank	he's	first	boy
use	fruit	plane	friend
planning	liked	kid	places
girl	kind	traffic	rule
didn't	blank	please	let's

Read the Story

Two girls were playing in their yard.

"Look," said the first girl. "There is a little bird on the sidewalk."

The other girl looked up in the tree. There was a nest on one of the branches.

"It fell from that tree," she said.

"This bird is not hurt, but I don't think it can fly," said the first girl.

"We could put it back in the nest," said the other girl.

They *climbed* up the tree and placed the little bird in the nest.

"That's better," they said together.

Read Carefully

think	I'll	her	lifting
sweep	sports	swept	candle
biking	both	hurt	live
or	handed	backing	shorts
juice	it's	thank	third
tennis	baking	goes	aren't
sweeping	for	handle	sleeping
couldn't	napkin	storm	thinking

Read the Story

The bike *parade* was yesterday morning. Traffic stopped for the bikes.

The bikes were *different* shapes, sizes, and *colors*.

Joan rode a pink bike with silver handlebars. Bill rode a red, white, and blue bike. He had a horn that beeped. Steve rode a black bike with gold stripes. He pulled his pet rabbit in a basket with wheels.

After the parade, the children had ice cream and cake.

"I wish we had a bike parade every day!" thought Steve.

Read Carefully

staring	cuddle	starting	for
sport	speck	thought	starring
grinning	hers	pickle	clothes
sleet	face	hasn't	gripping
color	picking	after	string
pumpkin	they're	stem	runner
turn	griping	shirt	scribble
steam	eyes	crosses	fur

Read the Story

A big crack of lightning flashed in the night sky! Rose sat up in her bed. She didn't like big thunderstorms. Rose cuddled next to Joy, her stuffed *bear.*

Mom came in and sat on Rose's bed. "I wanted to check on you," said Mom.

"I'm okay," said Rose, "but Joy is *afraid.*"

"I see," said Mom. "Why don't you tell Joy we need the rain? It fills up our lakes, rivers, and streams."

"Well," said Rose. "If the rain could be a little *quieter,* then maybe Joy wouldn't be so afraid!"

Read Carefully

tackle	dripping	head	surprise
dropped	there's	raking	porches
eight	piles	thought	pull
grilled	better	drifting	we'll
people	ice	turtle	join
under	cases	well	tickle
miles	sister	coin	only
driving	nibble	you've	ever

Read the Story

Postman Pete liked to play jokes. Today was Grandma Stone's birthday. She was waiting on her porch.

"Is there a letter or card for me?" asked Grandma Stone.

"Not one letter or card," said Postman Pete.

"Is there a *package*?"

"Not one package,"

"Oh, dear," sighed Grandma Stone. "No one remembered my birthday."

"Surprise!" said Postman Pete opening his bag. "You have lots of letters, cards, and packages!"

"Oh, Pete," said Grandma Stone, smiling. "You're such a tease!"

Read Carefully

race	string	drives	joking
you're	drove	more	never
spinning	school	piled	strong
people	shine	boy	places
spilled	letter	stacking	who's
shining	point	shell	toy
yesterday	drive	number	shone
spray	she'll	spring	almost

Read the Story

Jade lived in a big hotel. She was quite vain. She kept herself clean and spotless.

Jade nodded to all of the *guests*, but she wouldn't let them pet her.

Each morning, Jade ate a nice dish of tuna.

Each afternoon, Jade curled up on the front desk.

She liked to nap in the sun. People thought she was a *statue*!

At night, Jade slept in a basket with a soft blanket.

Do you know what Jade is? What were the clues?

Read Carefully

shipping	live	rule	new
color	shaped	sharp	walk
girl	lifted	few	happen
graded	thought	suit	too
once	finish	know	leave
shape	girls	left	food
knew	first	love	won't
grills	mule	born	bird

Read the Story

Today was the big car race. The bell rang! All the cars were off!

A blue car was fast, but a red car was faster. It was the fastest car on the track.

Cars wanted to get *ahead*, but the red car stayed in the lead.

The people cheered for the red car to win. There were just a few laps to go.

Then the blue car pulled *ahead*! It won the race!

"I knew I could do it," said the man in the blue car.

Read Carefully

riding	every	floating	soon
few	skating	her	himself
skipped	room	north	hurt
wash	tube	keep	love
fruit	third	eyes	new
limit	kind	there's	rides
peek	hoping	flew	those
clothes	hers	turn	tune

Read the Story

It was a cold Saturday morning. It had snowed the night before.

"We can't wait to go sledding," said the twins.

"First, you must eat *breakfast*," said Mom.

Mom gave each twin a dish of hot oatmeal with *sugar* and cream. The twins ate every spoonful.

Then Mom helped them put on snow pants and boots. They pulled on coats, hats, mittens, and scarves.

"Let's go," said the first twin.

"I can't *move*!" said the other twin. "I have on too many clothes!"

Read Carefully

shining	after	seen	walk
flute	sandbox	room	Sue
once	soon	throw	every
you'll	born	pull	strong
letter	twisting	flew	boom
singing	only	spoon	surprise
broom	twisted	threw	clever
corn	chew	better	both

Read the Story

Dolphins are little whales that swim in the *ocean*. They are strong swimmers. Dolphins can swim faster than people.

They dive deep into the ocean to find food. They eat *different* kinds of fish, such as cod. They can see under the ocean as well as you can see on land!

Dolphins love to jump. They can jump up as high as 20 feet!

Dolphins are thought to be *among* the brightest fish. They love to show off their tricks.

Have you ever seen a dolphin?

Read Carefully

torch	glowing	ever	park
comic	eight	she'd	flew
too	driving	walk	moon
flea	stew	boot	head
wash	June	yesterday	doesn't
never	dark	love	Sue
hiked	food	glowed	tooth
drew	porch	people	napkin

Read the Story

Nurse Kim is a good nurse. She takes care of her *patients*. Today she has people waiting to see her.

Jack is sick. His head is hot. Nurse Kim gives him a spoonful of liquid *medicine*.

"This tastes like grapes," said Jack.

Grandpa Tom has a cut on his leg. Nurse Kim washes the cut. She puts medicine on it. Then she wraps it up.

"Keep it clean and dry," she tells Grandpa Tom.

Nurse Kim took care of every patient.

"I love my job," she said.

Read Carefully

turtle	shining	those	modern
thrive	gloom	sprays	raccoon
every	short	shone	sister
grew	threw	hoop	aren't
unpack	school	under	once
number	kings	more	knight
spending	blue	three	sport
almost	don't	groom	blew

Read the Story

Basketball was Luke's *favorite* sport.

Luke's team *practiced* shooting hoops every day.

Once there was a big game at his school. Luke's team, the Turtles, played the Rabbits.

The Rabbits *laughed* at the Turtles.

"You are too slow," they said. The Rabbits ran everywhere. Each one wanted to be the strongest and quickest. They were rude to each other.

Luke's team played a nice, smooth game. They showed they were the better team. They won the game.

"I knew we could!" said Luke.

Read Carefully

house	today	proper	oil
number	bitten	more	surfing
trumpet	how	driver	puzzle
our	torches	turning	full
driving	suffer	now	river
panic	cow	finishing	wash
out	fishing	phrase	surfer
every	drives	few	down

Read the Story

Once upon a time, there was a greedy king.

"I will give a party," he said. "Everyone must bring me gold!"

On the day of the party, no one came. The king was sad.

Finally, a little girl came. She gave the king a gold flower.

"This is all that I have," she said. The king was *ashamed* of himself.

He gave another party. This time he didn't ask for gold. Everyone came.

The king found out it is better to give than to *receive*.

Read Carefully

jungle	found	coin	often
horn	longer	baker	modern
bursting	waited	early	brown
flattest	those	busted	banker
full	blanket	now	sandbox
round	juggle	limit	love
darkest	photograph	house	basket
flapped	today	dolphin	nephew

Read the Story

Betty loved her new purple cellphone.

One day she went shopping with a friend. They both spent money on clothes.

Suddenly, Betty couldn't find her phone. She looked around the store. She looked up and down the counters.

"I know!" said her friend. "I'll call your phone. That way, we'll know where it is."

Soon Betty could hear a soft ringing. Her phone was in one of her shopping bags.

"I was lucky this time," said Betty. "I will take better care of my phone from now on!"

Read Carefully

satin	gopher	joint	shorter
caring	walk	spotless	wake
full	stronger	early	cared
whirl	catch	stared	sound
cattle	lasting	money	card
only	robin	later	itch
rocket	town	longest	found
point	started	once	sport

Read the Story

February 2 is Groundhog Day. Many people think the groundhog can tell when it will be spring.

Crowds wait around early in the morning to see the groundhog. They are very *quiet* and try not to make a sound. They try to catch the groundhog when he comes out of his home.

If he sees his shadow, there will be six more weeks of winter.

If he doesn't see his shadow, then spring is on its way.

Read Carefully

today	dentist	coin	room
staring	thicker	nurse	solid
soon	ditch	thinker	around
simple	phonics	color	stirring
join	often	scribble	purse
starting	third	form	too
new	comic	thought	joy
brightest	birth	upset	match

Read the Story

Billy had the chicken pox. They were all over his tummy, and they really itched!

No one would come to his house to play. They didn't want to catch the chicken pox germs.

Billy was *covered* in a cream. It helped the itch, but he couldn't play on his *computer*. It would get greasy.

For a week Billy slept and tried not to scratch. *Finally*, the chicken pox were healed. Billy could play on his computer and with his friends. He was very happy!

Read Carefully

traffic	knew	moist	pebble
cleanest	packing	nerve	early
today	trapped	topic	storm
parking	full	stitch	barked
people	closer	paddle	food
clever	spoil	shopper	happen
latch	dolphin	pull	money
enjoy	curve	trapper	barking

Read the Story

The Miller *family* could hear a noise in their attic.

"Maybe there is a *squirrel* up there," said Dad.

"Please see what it is," said Mom.

Dad went up the attic ladder. He shined his flashlight. There were two big eyes looking back at him. It was a baby raccoon.

Dad got a cage with a strong latch and trapped the raccoon.

"Oh," said Mom. "He is such a cute and funny little *guy*."

That is how Rocky Raccoon came to live with the Miller family.

Read Carefully

crowded	older	study	look
baby	book	love	colder
though	wedding	circus	down
sixty	cooler	good	circle
higher	itches	weeding	water
tooth	crispy	walk	hurry
brown	teeth	camper	lighting
camped	warm	spout	took

Read the Story

There are few *pleasures* as great as a good book. A good book will transport you to a new place. It can take you places you've never been.

You can be a knight, a spy, or a *movie* star. You can ride on a rocket ship or sail the seven seas. You can be a camper in the woods or the *pilot* of a plane.

A good book will teach you many new things.

What are you waiting for? Grab a good book and start reading!

Read Carefully

mailing	cook	party	patch
once	planes	those	keeping
clown	pitches	cow	water
stood	frown	planning	hook
kept	though	foot	crown
colder	handy	tooth	found
every	mailed	flower	along
seated	wood	thought	shiny

Read the Story

Ladies and *gentlemen!* Children of all ages! Welcome
to the circus!

Thrill to the daring tricks on the high wire!

See the brave lion tamer enter a cage with the king of
the jungle!

Laugh along with the crazy clowns squirting water!

Look at all of the *beautiful* ponies prancing in a circle.

Watch the *acrobats* show their *amazing* skills!

Get your peanuts, popcorn, and *cotton* candy!

Hurry, hurry, and don't be late! Come on in, everyone.
It is the best show in town!

Name _____

Read Carefully

standing	age	shady	shook
warm	stitch	laugh	shaded
stopping	heard	ginger	large
house	flatter	cook	today
loud	people	switches	giraffe
pony	soaking	forty	purple
wash	now	full	how
floated	cages	proud	crook

Read the Story

George was a grumpy *giant* who lived in a large, smelly *castle*. George didn't like his smelly castle, so he went to town.

The town heard him coming because he shook the ground with his huge feet.

Babies cried. Dogs and cats howled. There was a town meeting to decide what to do.

The next day all of the townspeople went to George's castle. They *brought* mops and pails of water. They cleaned the castle top to *bottom*.

George was no longer grumpy. He liked staying home in his clean castle.

Read Carefully

patch	dropping	often	wood
book	age	city	stage
drooping	though	pages	our
penny	cooking	hood	water
heard	brook	count	strange
cooling	muddy	money	hook
out	along	smoother	only
brighter	match	change	quickest

Read the Story

Giraffes are the tallest *animals* living on land. They have long necks and spotted coats.

Male giraffes can *weigh* almost 3,000 pounds and be 19 feet tall. Female giraffes are around 16 feet tall and can weigh over 2,000 pounds.

Giraffes do not eat meat. Their long necks help them eat leaves on the highest branches. They can go for a few days without water.

Giraffes in the *wild travel* in large herds and live in *Africa.* They can live to be 25 years old.

Read Carefully

taking	round	laugh	catch
barge	water	hook	empty
crazy	stained	stood	around
heard	sound	lady	bridges
stacked	gem	warm	shout
shook	tower	latches	hood
early	pledge	ground	along
steaming	lazy	germ	town

Read the Story

"Please don't *touch* my loose tooth," said Beth. "It will hurt."

"Let me just look around a little," said Dr. Jones, the dentist. "Do you brush your teeth often?"

"I brush my teeth at least twice a day," said Beth.

"Good job, Beth!" said Dr. Jones. "Do you floss?"

"I floss my teeth every day," said Beth.

"Good job, Beth!" said Dr. Jones. "You can go."

"What about my loose tooth?" asked Beth.

"I *already* pulled it out," said Dr. Jones, holding up Beth's tooth.

"Good job, Dr. Jones!" said Beth.

Read Carefully

patches	drinking	saw	laugh
story	photograph	blinking	driving
blanks	wash	anything	stormy
wrapper	fifty	ball	pennies
nothing	also	panic	matches
taping	greedy	heard	those
cries	stories	sturdy	wrapping
satin	danger	bridge	all

Read the Story

It was *picture* day at school. The *second* grade class lined up on bleachers. Then Katy got the giggles. Soon all the second graders were giggling and laughing. Nothing the *photographer* did could make them stop. Then he had an idea.

"I want everyone to give me a silly face," he said.

Everyone made a very silly face.

"Now," he said, "All of you give me a nice smile."

Two weeks later the photographs came back. Everyone agreed the silly photograph was the best!

Read Carefully

coldest	softest	book	bumper
charges	call	soapy	fall
anything	satin	danger	dolphin
dried	every	draw	done
shouldn't	dirty	good	small
warm	softer	buddies	dirty
look	always	woman	along
haven't	change	bumped	took

Read the Story

I love to go to the *movies* with my friends. We like to go on Sunday afternoon.

We get our tickets at the ticket booth. Then we get salted popcorn, cold drinks, and candies. I like *chocolate* malt balls. We take plenty of napkins!

We like to sit in the row closest to the screen. Last week, we saw a movie about a dolphin. He was in danger and his buddies saved him. It was a good movie.

We can't wait until next Sunday afternoon!

Read Carefully

shaker	robin	large	water
punish	work	candies	river
shack	cried	done	stood
nothing	fighter	page	crawl
locker	shake	crying	huge
drawn	thickest	though	full
emptied	word	shaking	strongest
longer	shook	shopper	laundry

Read the Story

"We're out of laundry soap," said Mom. "Danny, please ride your bike to the store and get some soap."

Danny rode his bike to the store and went inside. He found the soap and went to the counter to pay.

"That will be $4.78, please," said the clerk.

Danny reached in his pocket, but there was no money. He started to panic. *Suddenly* he *remembered* he'd put the money in his *shoe* so it wouldn't get lost!

Danny paid for the soap and took it to his mom.

Read Carefully

babies	thirsty	wishing	cities
scratch	sauce	woman	world
anything	neater	flies	hood
scrape	today	thirty	money
wooden	filed	worst	malt
gentle	salt	around	stage
filled	nesting	switching	launch
scraps	worth	hook	thicker

Read the Story

You can tell a robin by its reddish *orange* chest. Male birds are more *colorful* than females.

When robins sing, it sounds like a *whistle*. They like to sing in the morning and late afternoon.

A female robin does her nesting up high where it will be safe. The nest is about 4 to 6 inches wide. Robin's eggs are light blue and are about the size of a quarter. Baby robins cannot fly until they are bigger.

Robins like to eat *berries*, worms, and insects.

Read Carefully

camper	scares	shady	wouldn't
anything	ladies	worship	woman
scars	charge	scared	shaded
shape	done	overlook	snowball
germ	tired	change	shiny
often	mall	early	nothing
tried	broken	shade	haul
brook	gem	faucet	hurried

Read the Story

Our scout troop went camping in the woods. We set up our tents. We hauled water from the brook for cooking and cleaning.

When we were done, we *built* a big fire. We roasted hot dogs and *marshmallows*. We were telling ghost stories when we heard a strange noise.

"I don't think there is anything to be scared of," said our scout leader.

Just then, a skunk hurried out of the woods. That was the end of our camping trip!

Read Carefully

drawn	tablecloth	writer	done
chimes	creepy	drew	work
fault	drain	another	braked
explain	talk	shadow	anything
darker	peaches	take	salty
pinch	nothing	faucet	fall
through	player	highway	space
moment	flatten	walk	word

Read the Story

The Andrews were driving down the highway when they hit a bump.

"The highway is getting bumpier," said Mr. Andrews.

"This is the bumpiest road ever," said Mrs. Andrews. "Maybe we should take another *route*."

Mr. Andrews braked and got off the highway. They drove through small towns and *villages*. They stopped to buy peaches at a fruit stand. At noon Mrs. Andrews *spread* a tablecloth on the grass for a picnic. At last they reached their *vacation* hotel.

"What a *pleasant* trip!" said Mrs. Andrews.

Read Carefully

zero	pillow	roasted	worry
noodle	today	cooked	supreme
smell	toaster	together	stable
sure	water	hooks	baseball
staple	birthday	hero	woman
worship	once	small	knock
princess	shook	thrown	basketball
joint	knocked	poodle	warm

Read the Story

Charlie liked working in a restaurant, but he was very clumsy.

On *Monday*, he spilled a bowl of noodles. On Tuesday, he knocked a water glass onto a woman's lap. On *Wednesday*, a birthday cake slipped off his tray onto the floor. On Thursday, he tried working in the kitchen but he almost set the place on fire. On Friday, Charlie and the owner talked.

"I sure like being in restaurants," said Charlie. "What can I do?"

"Maybe the best job for you is being the *customer*," said the owner.

Charlie decided that was the best job for him!

Use with Lesson 72

Read Carefully

bridges	foolish	wash	stood
call	worth	wires	often
taken	another	hood	folded
birdcage	fallen	world	chalk
boyhood	crawl	through	bundle
together	fooled	problem	full
proper	word	bugle	oatmeal
flood	broken	took	worst

Read the Story

Come to the Spiffy Car Wash!

Bring us your dirtiest, smelliest cars and trucks. We'll make them spiffy clean.

We *vacuum* up the dirt and *crumbs* on the seats and *floors*.

We wash the dirt off the hood and the bugs off the grill.

We scrub the tires and polish the body to a *beautiful* wax shine.

When we're through, your cars and trucks will look brand new.

Bring your cars and trucks to us today! We're sure you will be *satisfied* with our work.

Read Carefully

spoil	quit	piling	oyster
quite	heard	large	early
through	studied	walnut	away
hawk	around	stitches	though
flew	perhaps	together	every
laugh	always	student	notebook
athlete	spilling	follow	love
ginger	sure	lawn	summer

Read the Story

Exercise, together with eating right, is sure to help you stay fit. You will feel good during the day. You will sleep better at night.

Student athletes exercise by playing sports. Basketball and swimming are good ways to exercise. Playing sports makes you strong.

Another way to stay fit is to eat right. Fruits, *vegetables*, and milk are part of a *healthy* diet. Meat, fish, and grains are also good. Limit *sugar* to just once in a while.

What are your plans to stay fit and *healthy*?

Read Carefully

spider	barge	middle	together
along	minus	though	twinkle
hotel	branches	cages	salt
crawl	through	sticking	sure
magic	eardrum	thaw	wrong
sticky	also	money	fault
another	wrinkle	ladybug	those
quizzes	bugle	thought	stages

Read the Story

One day a man stumbled over a magic lamp. He rubbed the lamp and out popped a *genie*.

"You may have three wishes," said the genie.

"I want to be clever at building things," he said.

In a twinkle the genie turned him into a spider.

"I sure don't want to be a spider!" said the man.

The genie turned him back into a man.

"One last wish," said the genie.

The man thought for a while.

"I know," he said. "I wish for three more wishes!"

Read Carefully

handier	walrus	share	popcorn
coaster	spool	babies	squirt
tries	early	garden	hungrier
surround	understand	should	scars
about	happiest	voice	square
argument	scold	harpoon	crawl
rocket	happen	around	showed
center	toaster	decide	return

Read the Story

My Grandma has a big flower garden. She works in her garden every day. She has many *lovely* flowers. There are red and pink roses. There are white and purple *petunias*.

I like to help in the garden. We squirt stuff on the flowers to get rid of the beetles. We dig up the weeds and plant new flowers.

Grandma says she is happiest when surrounded by beautiful flowers.

I decided that when I grow up, I want a big garden, too.

Read Carefully

juggle	repeat	decide	struggle
muddiest	uglier	sports	bumpier
waltz	lunch	water	pilot
spout	greedier	umpire	flies
along	wrapper	luckier	golden
launch	perhaps	paper	greasiest
jungle	yesterday	though	spotted
skinnier	done	round	beetle

Read the Story

On fall afternoons the kids on my street enjoy playing football. We play in the park near our homes. It is a friendly game, and we all have a good time.

Jack is big. He likes to tackle. Tom is the fastest runner. *Chris* has the best arm and can throw the football a long way. We *challenge* each other to see who can get the muddiest.

Playing sports is a *wonderful* way to spend time with your friends.

Read Carefully

emptied	hundred	happier	forest
hurries	funniest	plowing	almighty
together	pillow	beside	mistake
unhappy	written	sure	yesterday
another	kneel	windiest	ugliest
teaspoon	happiest	summer	laugh
winter	knuckle	dried	include
knelt	woman	teacher	parties

Read the Story

Emma and Jan were spending the week at a horse ranch. They would learn to ride and care for horses.

"Howdy, pardners," said Cowboy Chuck. "Welcome to Maple Rock Ranch."

Emma's horse was named Majesty. He was black with white markings. Jan's horse was a chestnut mare named Zipper. She liked to go fast.

Emma and Jan spent the first day riding their horses. By evening they were very sore.

"I think tomorrow I'll look for a horse named Pillow!" exclaimed Jan.

Read Carefully

swollen	remember	zone	cried
struggle	kitties	pounds	expand
bumpiest	twice	pencil	further
exclaim	stirring	foggier	anything
cities	heard	string	starring
electric	moment	phrase	majesty
modern	foggiest	shadow	fingers
another	hurried	clumsier	yolk

Read the Story

Saving water helps everyone. There are many ways to save water.

Don't let water run while you are brushing your teeth.

Take short showers *instead* of long baths.

Ask a parent to check the water meter at your house.
A broken water meter will leak and waste water.

Dishwashers should be full before you run them. Washing *machines* should also be full.

Water your lawn only twice a week.

Remember, it just takes a moment to save *gallons* of water.

Read Carefully

northern	fifteenth	thought	stories
became	inches	suggested	remain
though	student	bumblebee	joined
bamboo	silent	shouted	hunting
seventeenth	settled	buzzes	sixteenth
single	nothing	bringing	through
supply	except	simple	clumsiest
burning	price	expect	belong

Read the Story

It was the last day of school. Mrs. Potts and her class were cleaning up the classroom. They stacked the books on the shelf and cleaned off the *boards*. The students put all their papers and pictures in big bags. When they finished, there were still two hours to go.

"We have nothing to do!" said the students.

"Surprise!" said Mrs. Potts. She brought out drinks and treats.

They read stories together, laughed, and had a good time.

It was a perfect way to end the school year.

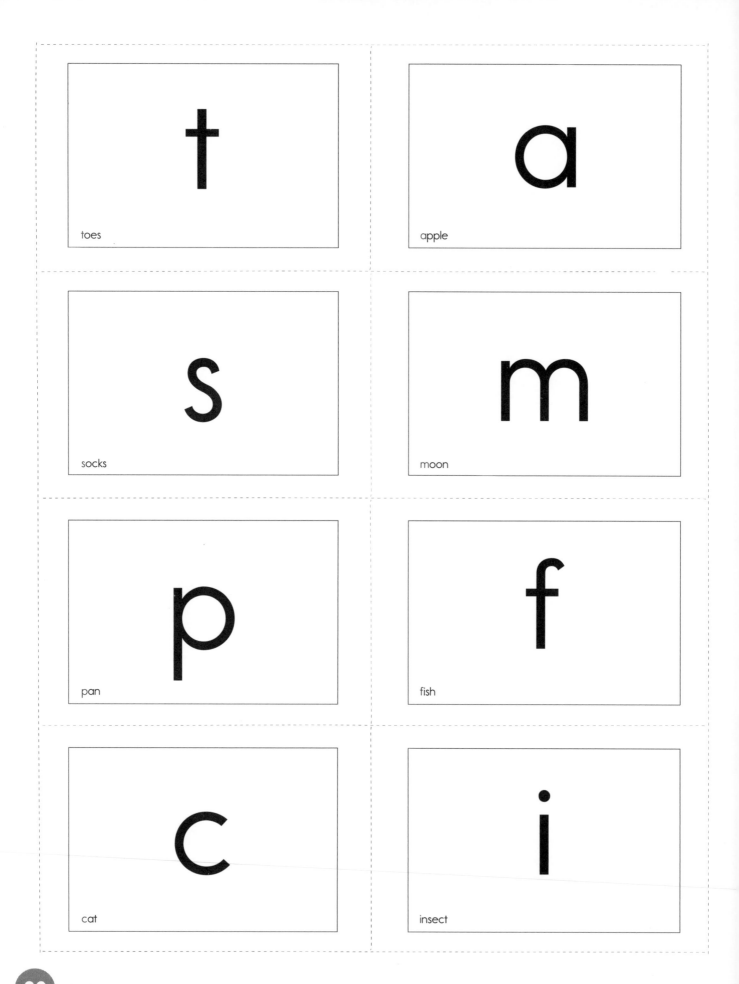

t

toes

a

apple

s

socks

m

moon

p

pan

f

fish

c

cat

i

insect

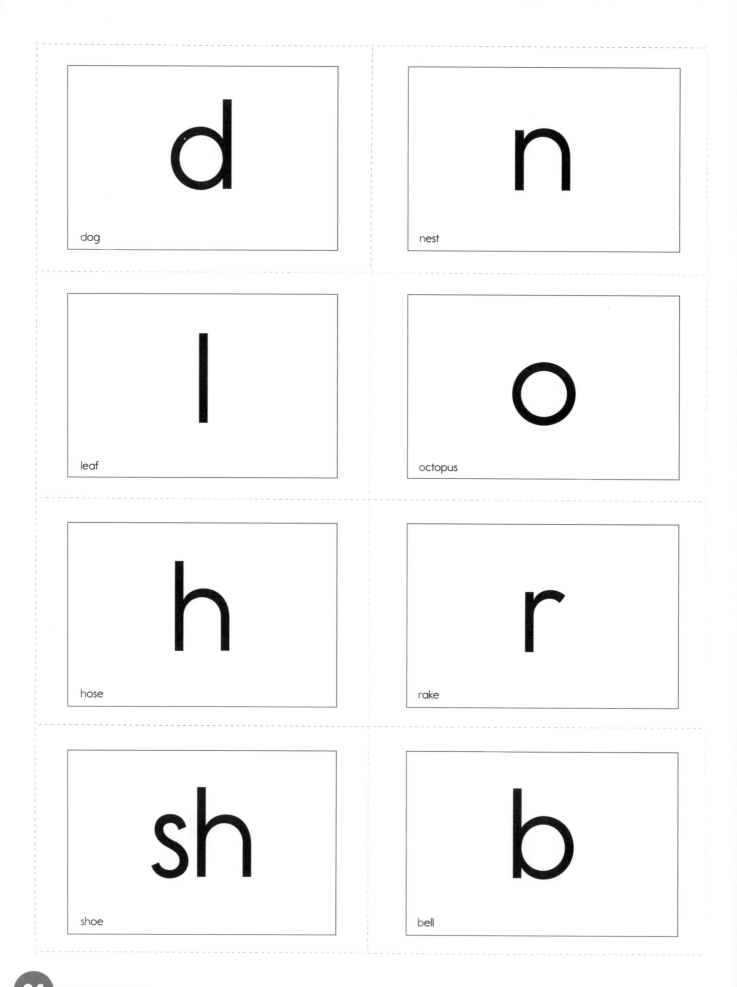

d

dog

n

nest

l

leaf

o

octopus

h

hose

r

rake

sh

shoe

b

bell

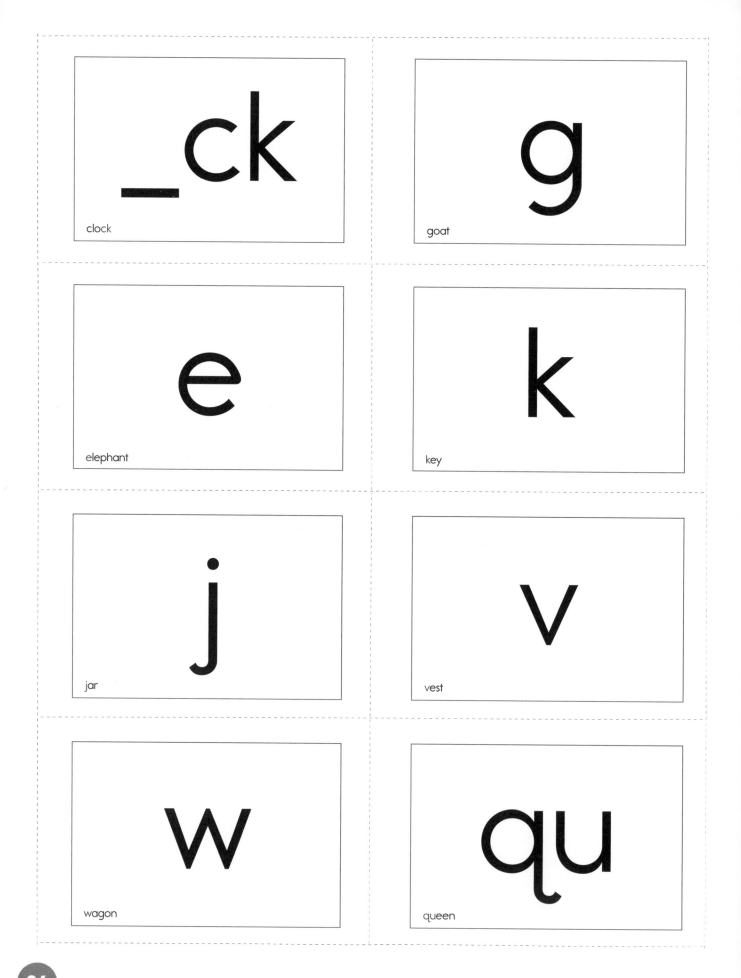

_ck

clock

g

goat

e

elephant

k

key

j

jar

v

vest

w

wagon

qu

queen

x

xray

th

thumb

z

zebra

y

yarn

ch

chair

u

umbrella

ai

train

a_e

cake

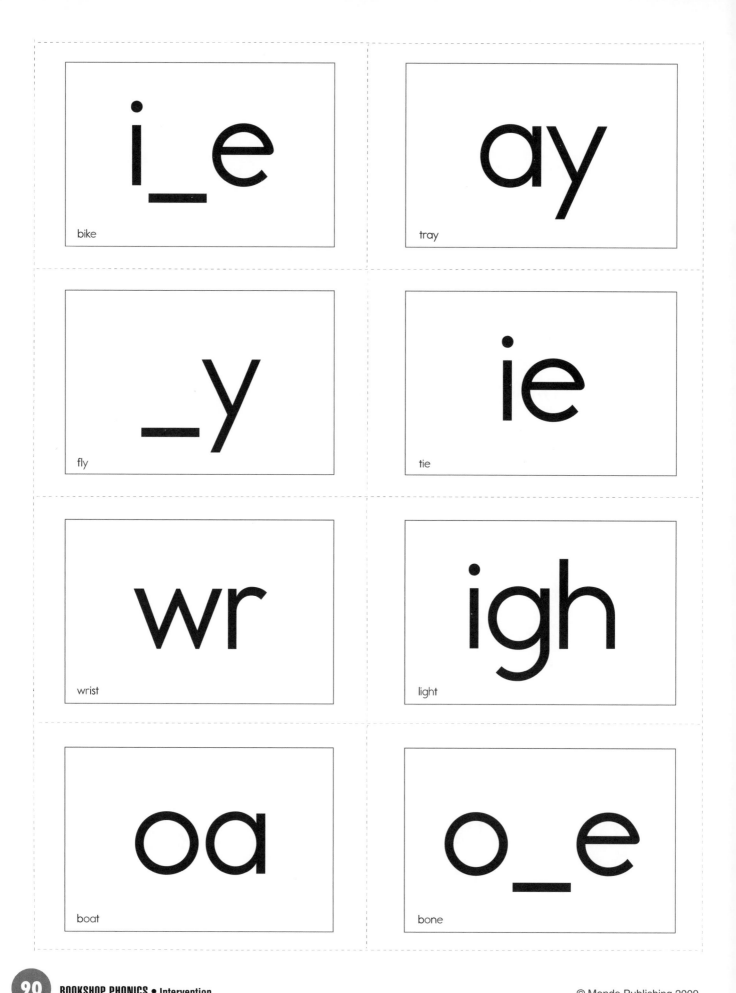

i_e

bike

ay

tray

_y

fly

ie

tie

wr

wrist

igh

light

oa

boat

o_e

bone

ow

bow

ol

gold

gn

sign

kn

knot

ee

feet

e_e

eve

ce

cent

ea

peach

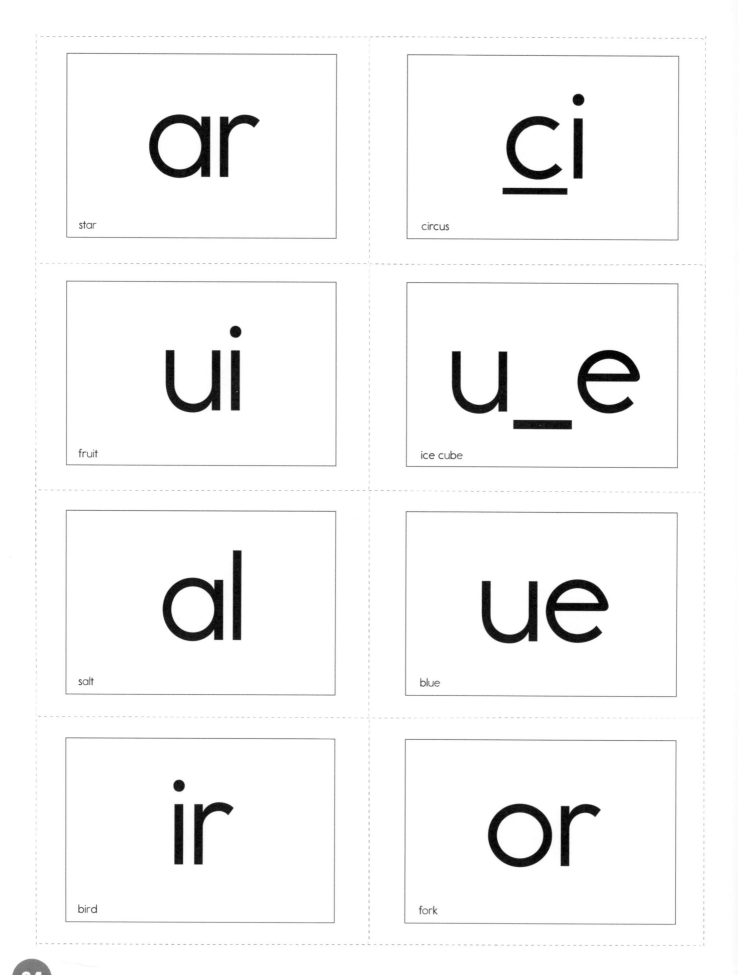

ar

star

ci

circus

ui

fruit

u_e

ice cube

al

salt

ue

blue

ir

bird

or

fork

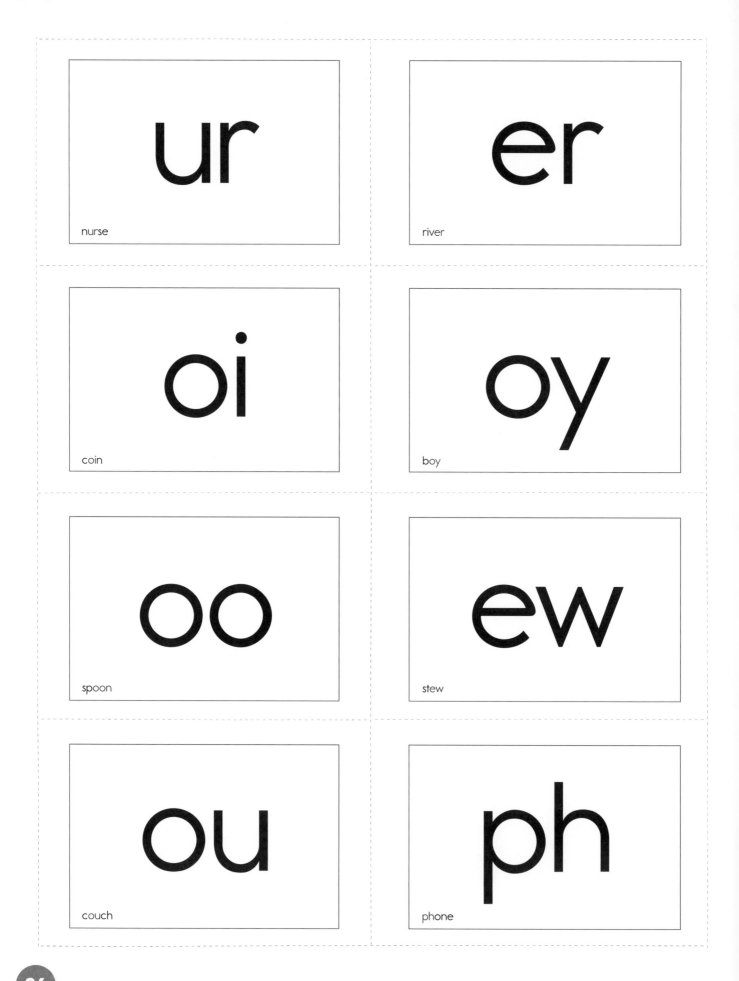

ur

nurse

er

river

oi

coin

oy

boy

oo

spoon

ew

stew

ou

couch

ph

phone

_tch

watch

ow

cow

ge

cage

oo

book

_dge

edge

gi

giraffe

aw

faucet

au

saw

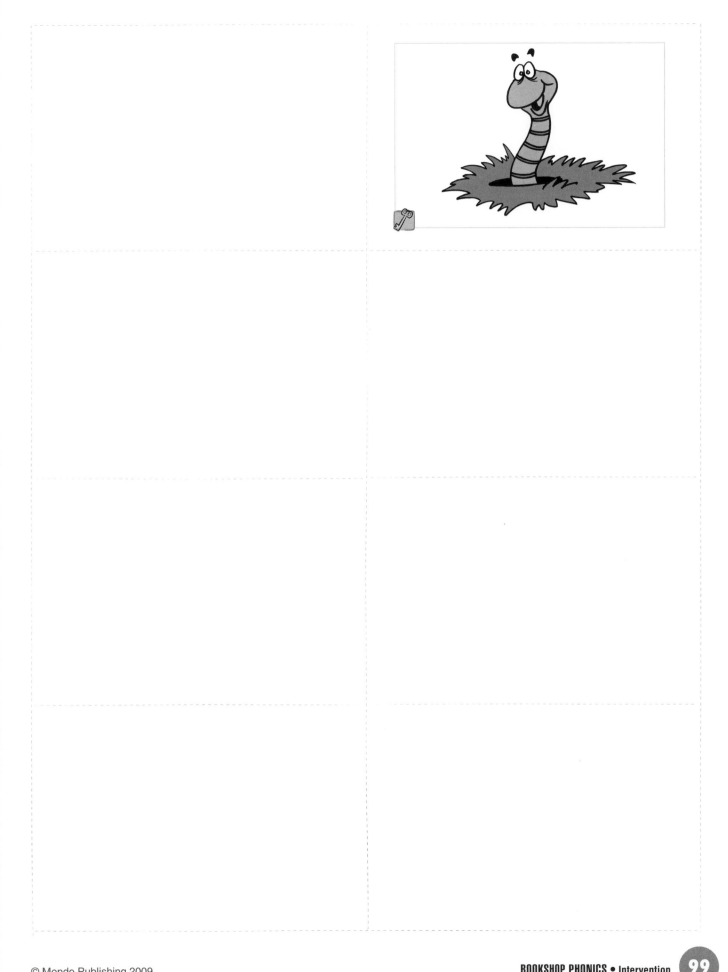

wor

worm

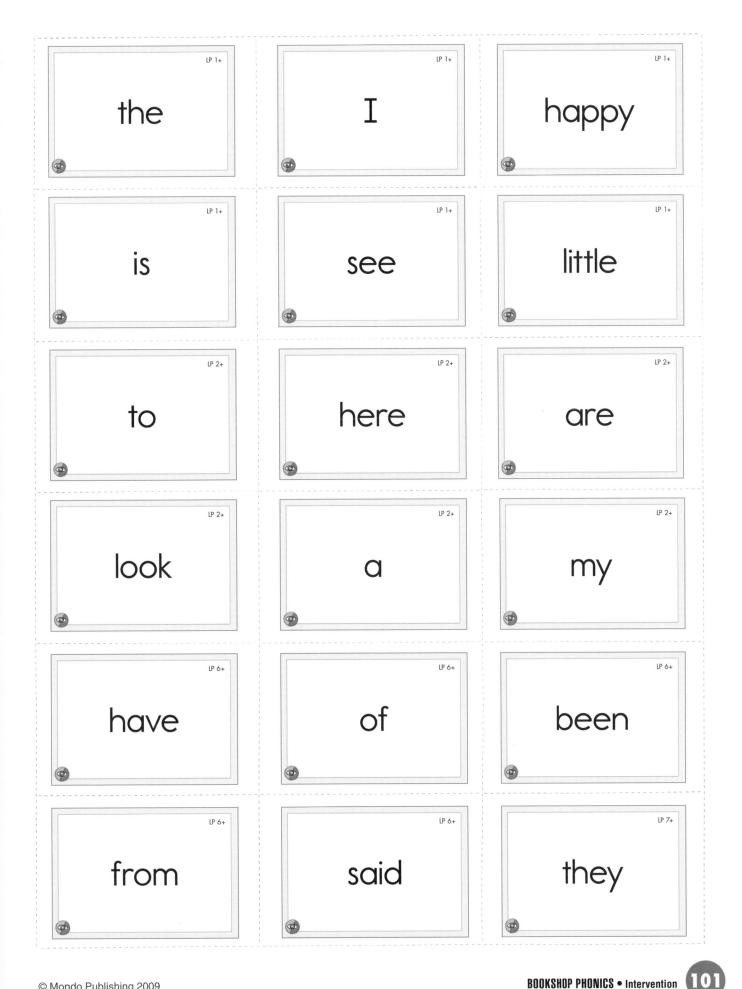

the

I

happy

is

see

little

to

here

are

look

a

my

have

of

been

from

said

they

has LP 7+	were LP 7+	you LP 7+
come LP 7+	does LP 11+	any LP 11+
there LP 11+	put LP 11+	like LP 11+
was LP 12+	who LP 12+	good LP 12+
do LP 12+	want LP 12+	your LP 16+
find LP 16+	as LP 16+	very LP 16+

their *LP 27+*	into *LP 27+*	please *LP 27+*
why *LP 27+*	would *LP 31+*	could *LP 31+*
should *LP 31+*	both *LP 32+*	buy *LP 32+*
hers *LP 32+*	live *LP 36+*	kind *LP 36+*
most *LP 36+*	goes *LP 37+*	friend *LP 37+*
o'clock *LP 37+*	almost *LP 41+*	head *LP 41+*

eyes LP 41+	school LP 42+	eight LP 42+
clothes LP 42+	more LP 46+	only LP 46+
color LP 46+	people LP 47+	pull LP 47+
thought LP 47+	once LP 51+	walk LP 51+
love LP 51+	every LP 52+	those LP 52+
wash LP 52+	full LP 56+	today LP 56+

© Mondo Publishing 2009

often LP 56+	early LP 57+	money LP 57+
around LP 57+	water LP 61+	though LP 61+
warm LP 61+	along LP 62+	heard LP 62+
laugh LP 62+	anything LP 66+	nothing LP 66+
done LP 67+	woman LP 67+	another LP 71+
through LP 71+	together LP 72+	sure LP 72+

are	happy	here
I	is	little
look	my	see
the	to	at
am	and	cat
fast	map	Sam

a	from	is
has	the	bag
band	big	cap
dog	gift	had
hand	hid	in
lost	Tim	Tom

here	I	is
like	my	put
the	bed	bells
box	dish	in
jam	Jan	left
that	this	with

can 16-20	come 16-20	his 16-20
is 16-20	the 16-20	the 16-20
where 16-20	in 16-20	jump 16-20
kitten 16-20	mitten 16-20	mud 16-20
rabbit 16-20	Stan 16-20	stick 16-20
stuck 16-20	us 16-20	with 16-20

a	a	t	t	m
m	s	s	f	f
p	p	p	i	i
c	c	n	n	d
d	d	o	o	l

l	r	r	h	h
b	b	sh	sh	g
g	ck	ck	k	k
e	e	v	v	j
j	qu	qu	w	w

th	th	x	x	y
y	z	z	u	u
ch	ch	a_e	a_e	ai
ai	ay	ay	i_e	i_e
ie	ie	_y	_y	igh

igh	wr	wr	o_e	o_e
oa	oa	ol	ol	ow
ow	kn	kn	gn	gn
e_e	e_e	ee	ee	ea
ea	ce	ce	ci	ci

ar	ar	u_e	u_e	ui
ui	ue	ue	al	al
or	or	ir	ir	er
er	ur	ur	oy	oy
oi	oi	ew	ew	oo

oo	ph	ph	ou	ou
ow	ow	_tch	_tch	oo
oo	ge	ge	gi	gi
_dge	_dge	au	au	aw
aw	wor	wor		